The ChatGPT Handbook

PA BOOKS

Published by PA BOOKS, 2023.

While every precaution has been taken in the preparation of this book, the publisher assumes no responsibility for errors or omissions, or for damages resulting from the use of the information contained herein.

THE CHATGPT HANDBOOK

First edition. October 21, 2023.

ISBN: 979-8223420927

Written by PA BOOKS.

Table of Contents

Introduction

Welcome to "The Ultimate Guide to ChatGPT"!

In this guidebook, we aim to provide you with a comprehensive understanding of ChatGPT and empower you to harness its capabilities effectively. Whether you are a curious individual, a developer, a business professional, or anyone interested in exploring the possibilities of AI-powered conversation, this guide is designed to help you get started, understand the technology, and use ChatGPT to its full potential.

Purpose of this Guide:

The purpose of this guidebook is threefold:

Inform: We'll introduce you to the world of ChatGPT, helping you grasp the underlying technology, its features, and its applications. You'll learn how ChatGPT fits into the broader landscape of artificial intelligence and natural language processing.

Empower: We'll equip you with the knowledge and skills needed to access and use ChatGPT effectively, whether you're interacting with it through web interfaces, integrating it into your applications using APIs, or exploring it through third-party applications.

Inspire: We'll showcase real-world applications and provide insights into best practices for using ChatGPT responsibly, ethically, and to its full potential. Our goal is to inspire you to explore creative and innovative uses of ChatGPT in your personal or professional endeavours.

What to Expect:

As you navigate through this guide, you can expect to find:

Clear instructions on how to get started with ChatGPT, whether you're using web interfaces, APIs, or applications.

An exploration of the capabilities and limitations of ChatGPT to help you understand what it can and cannot do.

Practical tips for effective communication with ChatGPT, including how to frame your queries and prompts.

A deep dive into advanced features, enabling you to tailor ChatGPT's responses to your specific needs.

Insightful guidance on responsible use, ethical considerations, and the mitigation of potential biases.

Real-world examples and case studies that demonstrate how ChatGPT is being used across various industries and domains.

A glossary of AI-related terms to help you navigate the technology's terminology.

References to additional resources for those looking to delve even deeper into AI and ChatGPT.

Chapter 1: Getting Started

In this chapter, we will guide you through the initial steps of accessing and using ChatGPT. Whether you plan to use it through web interfaces, APIs, or applications, this section will help you get started on your journey with ChatGPT.

1.1 Accessing ChatGPT:

ChatGPT can be accessed through various methods, and the choice depends on your specific needs and preferences. Here are the most common ways:

a. Web Interfaces:

Many organizations and platforms provide web-based access to ChatGPT. Simply visit their websites and follow the on-screen instructions to start a conversation. You may need to create an account or subscribe to a service to access the full features.

b. APIs (Application Programming Interfaces):

For developers and businesses looking to integrate ChatGPT into their applications, OpenAI offers APIs. These APIs allow you to interact with ChatGPT programmatically, enabling custom solutions for a wide range of applications.

c. Applications:

Some third-party applications and chatbots have integrated ChatGPT into their systems. Download and install these applications, and you can communicate with ChatGPT seamlessly.

1.2 Account Setup:

Depending on the method you choose, you may need to set up an account:

a. Web Interfaces:

If you're using a web interface, sign up for an account if required. Follow the registration process, including providing your email address, creating a password, and agreeing to the terms of use.

b. APIs:

To use ChatGPT through an API, you will need to sign up with OpenAI and obtain an API key. Detailed instructions for this process can usually be found in OpenAI's documentation or developer resources.

1.3 Basic Usage:

After you've gained access to ChatGPT, you're ready to start using it. Here are the fundamental steps for initiating a conversation:

a. Web Interfaces:

Log in to your account.

Find the ChatGPT interface.

Start a new conversation or join an existing one.

Begin typing your queries or prompts, and ChatGPT will respond accordingly.

b. APIs:

Developers will integrate the API into their applications using the provided API key.

Send HTTP requests to the API endpoint with the necessary parameters, like your text input.

The API will return ChatGPT's response, which you can then display in your application.

1.4 Tips for Effective Communication:

When interacting with ChatGPT, provide clear and specific instructions.

Feel free to experiment with different prompts to achieve the desired output.

Be patient, as the quality of responses may vary based on the complexity of your requests.

1.5 Security and Privacy:

Keep in mind that some platforms may store the conversations you have with ChatGPT.

Be cautious about sharing sensitive or personal information in your interactions.

With these initial steps, you're well on your way to utilizing ChatGPT effectively. The subsequent chapters will delve deeper into understanding ChatGPT, exploring advanced features, and applying it in various real-world scenarios.

Chapter 2: Understanding ChatGPT

In this chapter, we will delve into the fascinating world of ChatGPT, breaking down the technology that powers it, its capabilities, and its limitations. By the end of this chapter, you'll have a clearer understanding of what ChatGPT can and cannot do, as well as an appreciation for the GPT-3.5 architecture that underpins it.

2.1 Technology behind ChatGPT:

ChatGPT is built on a foundation of deep learning and natural language processing, which are two key components of artificial intelligence. Here's an overview of the technology that powers ChatGPT:

Deep Learning:

ChatGPT's core technology is deeply rooted in the field of deep learning, a subset of artificial intelligence. Deep learning models, inspired by the human brain, consist of layers of artificial neurons that process and learn from vast amounts of data. In the case of ChatGPT, the specific neural network architecture employed is known as the Transformer.

The Transformer architecture revolutionized the field of natural language processing (NLP) when it was introduced. It's particularly adept at processing sequences of data, making it ideal for tasks like language understanding and generation. The Transformer's design involves two key components: the encoder and the decoder, which work together to process and generate text.

The Encoder: This component processes the input text, breaking it down into a series of embedding's, each representing a word or token. The encoder's self-attention mechanism allows it to weigh the importance of different words in the input, considering the context and relationships between them. This process enables ChatGPT to understand the structure and nuances of human language.

The Decoder: The decoder, on the other hand, takes the information from the encoder and generates text based on that understanding. It generates one word or token at a time, considering what has been generated so far and the input data. This process results in coherent, human-like text responses.

Deep learning and the Transformer architecture have enabled ChatGPT to mimic human language understanding and generation to an impressive degree. It can grasp context, syntax, semantics, and even certain aspects of reasoning, allowing it to provide contextually relevant and coherent responses to a wide range of prompts and queries.

However, while ChatGPT's deep learning foundation enables it to produce human-like text, it's important to keep in mind that it doesn't possess true understanding or consciousness. Instead, it relies on patterns in the data it was trained on to generate responses, which means its responses are limited to the knowledge and patterns present in its training data. This leads to both its remarkable capabilities and its limitations, which we'll explore further in this guide.

Pre-trained Models:

ChatGPT's proficiency in language comprehension and generation is largely attributed to its extensive pre-training on a vast and diverse dataset sourced from the internet. This pre-training process plays a pivotal role in equipping ChatGPT with the foundational knowledge and language skills that it leverages to produce meaningful and contextually relevant responses.

Vast Dataset: The pre-training phase of ChatGPT exposes the model to an immense corpus of text, encompassing a wide range of subjects, styles, and sources from the internet. This extensive dataset includes articles, books, websites, forums, and more. It's this broad exposure that allows ChatGPT to develop a versatile understanding of language and a general knowledge base.

Learning Grammar: Through this exposure, ChatGPT learns the intricacies of grammar, syntax, and language structure. It becomes proficient at forming coherent sentences, identifying parts of speech, and recognizing grammatical rules.

Factual Knowledge: The vast dataset also introduces ChatGPT to a wealth of factual information. This includes historical facts, scientific principles, current events, and a wide array of trivia. As a result, ChatGPT can provide answers to factual questions and even perform basic calculations.

Reasoning Abilities: While ChatGPT doesn't possess true reasoning abilities like a human, its pre-training equips it with the capacity to make inferences and draw logical conclusions based on patterns it has learned. It can use this skill to generate responses that follow a logical train of thought.

Common-Sense Knowledge: The dataset also imparts common-sense knowledge that is often assumed in human communication. ChatGPT can understand and apply everyday common-sense reasoning, making its responses more contextually relevant and coherent.

The pre-training phase serves as the foundation upon which ChatGPT builds its conversational capabilities. It acts as a language model that has learned to predict the next word in a sentence based on the context and data it has seen during its training. However, it's essential to keep in mind that ChatGPT's responses are generated based on patterns in the data it was exposed to during pre-training, which means it might not always have access to the most up-to-date information or specialized knowledge.

Understanding ChatGPT's pre-training process provides insight into how it processes and generates text, as well as why it may excel in some areas while occasionally falling short in others. This foundation allows ChatGPT to be a powerful tool for a variety of applications, from content creation to natural language understanding and beyond.

Fine-tuning:

Fine-tuning is a critical phase in the development of ChatGPT, following its initial pre-training on a vast dataset. This phase involves refining the model's behaviour and responses to make it safer, controlled, and aligned with specific use cases. It ensures that ChatGPT can be employed in a responsible and effective manner for a wide range of applications.

Narrower Dataset: During fine-tuning, ChatGPT is exposed to a narrower dataset that has been carefully curated to align with particular requirements and guidelines. This dataset might contain examples of desirable behaviour and responses, as well as counterexamples that illustrate behaviour to avoid. By using a narrower dataset, fine-tuning narrows the models focus and tailors it to specific applications.

Human Reviewers: Human reviewers play a central role in the fine-tuning process. They are provided with guidelines by OpenAI that outline the expectations for the model's behaviour. These guidelines emphasize responsible AI use, avoiding harmful content, and maintaining neutrality and respect. Human reviewers review and rate model outputs for various inputs, helping the model learn to produce the desired responses.

Iterative Process: Fine-tuning is an iterative process that involves continuous feedback and adjustments. Human reviewers provide feedback on the model's responses, and OpenAI maintains a strong feedback loop with them to address questions, clarify guidelines, and refine the model's behaviour over time.

Balancing Act: Fine-tuning represents a delicate balance. It seeks to preserve the model's usefulness while ensuring it adheres to safety and ethical standards. Striking this balance is essential to avoid overcorrection, which might stifle the model's creativity, and to prevent under correction, which could allow harmful or inappropriate content.

Specific Use Cases: The fine-tuning process is adaptable to different use cases and requirements. For example, fine-tuning for a chatbot used in customer support will differ from fine-tuning for an educational application or content generation tool. By customizing the fine-tuning process, ChatGPT can be tailored for specific applications.

2.2 Capabilities:

ChatGPT's capabilities are both impressive and versatile:

Conversational:

ChatGPT's ability to engage in dynamic text-based conversations is one of its most notable features, making it a versatile tool for a variety of applications, including chatbots, virtual assistants, and customer support. Let's explore this conversational capability in more depth:

Real-Time Interaction: ChatGPT is designed to interact with users in real time. This means it can respond to a user's input immediately, creating the sense of a natural and engaging conversation. Whether you're asking questions, seeking assistance, or simply engaging in casual chat, ChatGPT is adept at maintaining the flow of conversation.

Multi-Turn Conversations: ChatGPT can handle multi-turn conversations, where the context of the conversation evolves as the exchange progresses. It can remember and reference prior messages, allowing for more meaningful and context-aware interactions.

Customizable Persona: In some implementations, ChatGPT can be assigned a persona or role, adapting its responses to a specific character or style. For instance, it can simulate the persona of a helpful assistant, a knowledgeable expert, or even a fictional character, making it suitable for a wide range of use cases.

Contextual Understanding: ChatGPT has the capacity to understand and adapt to the conversation's context. It can comprehend user queries based on previous messages, providing responses that remain contextually relevant.

Natural Language Processing: One of ChatGPT's strengths is its natural language processing abilities. It can understand and generate human-like text, making the conversation feel more intuitive and approachable. This is especially valuable when creating user-friendly interfaces and chatbots.

Customer Support: Many organizations employ ChatGPT to bolster their customer support operations. ChatGPT can assist customers with common queries, direct them to relevant resources, or even troubleshoot common issues, thereby improving customer satisfaction and reducing the burden on human support agents.

Virtual Assistants: In the realm of virtual assistants, ChatGPT can serve as a helpful, text-based assistant. It can set reminders, answer questions, provide recommendations, or carry out various tasks based on user instructions.

Chatbots: ChatGPT is often used as the foundation for chatbots across industries. These chatbots can be found on websites, messaging apps, and customer service platforms, serving diverse functions, from information retrieval to guiding users through processes.

Content Generation:

ChatGPT's remarkable capability to generate content is a testament to its versatility and usefulness. It excels at creating a wide range of text, making it a valuable tool for various content-related tasks, including article writing, marketing materials, creative writing, and more.

Article Writing: ChatGPT can assist in generating articles on a multitude of topics. Whether you're a content creator looking to streamline the writing process or a researcher seeking drafts for in-depth articles, ChatGPT can produce well-structured and coherent content.

Marketing Materials: Businesses often leverage ChatGPT to craft marketing content, including product descriptions, ad copy, and promotional material. The model can adapt its writing style to suit different marketing strategies, such as informative, persuasive, or engaging content.

Creative Writing: For authors, poets, and creative writers, ChatGPT serves as a valuable source of inspiration. It can offer creative prompts, generate short stories, or even assist in brainstorming ideas for novels, scripts, or other creative projects.

SEO Content: ChatGPT can create search engine optimized (SEO) content by incorporating keywords and phrases that improve a piece's visibility on search engines. This is particularly beneficial for content creators and website owners aiming to enhance their online presence.

Technical Writing: When it comes to producing technical documents, manuals, or guides, ChatGPT can provide clear, concise, and well-structured content. It aids in communicating complex information in an understandable manner.

Academic and Research Writing: For students and researchers, ChatGPT can be a helpful tool in generating drafts, summaries, or explanations of academic papers and research findings. It can also assist in the development of thesis statements and research proposals.

Content Ideas: If you're in need of fresh ideas or topics, ChatGPT can offer suggestions and brainstorming assistance. It can help you identify trending subjects, evergreen topics, or niche themes.

Language Translation:

ChatGPT is proficient at translating content from one language to another, making it a versatile tool for creating multilingual content.

Language Translation: ChatGPT's ability to facilitate language translation is a testament to its versatility and its potential to foster global communication and understanding. This feature makes it a valuable tool for bridging language barriers, whether in personal or professional contexts.

Multilingual Communication: ChatGPT can proficiently translate text from one language to another. This enables individuals, businesses, and organizations to engage in multilingual communication, extending their reach to audiences around the world.

Global Business: In the realm of international business, ChatGPT serves as a powerful asset for companies looking to expand their operations and reach a global clientele. It can assist in translating marketing materials, product descriptions, and customer support communications into various languages.

Cultural Exchange: For personal use, ChatGPT can be a valuable companion for travellers, students, and individuals interested in cultural exchange. It allows you to engage with people from different linguistic backgrounds, fostering connections and broadening horizons.

Education and Research: ChatGPT aids students and researchers in accessing and understanding content in languages other than their own. It simplifies the process of exploring academic papers, books, and resources in different languages, promoting academic exchange.

Humanitarian Aid and Crisis Response: During humanitarian crises, ChatGPT's language translation capabilities become indispensable for communication between aid workers and affected communities. It helps ensure that critical information and assistance are accessible to those in need.

Breaking down Barriers: Language barriers often hinder communication and collaboration. ChatGPT's translation abilities contribute to breaking down these barriers, allowing people to engage with others regardless of the languages they speak.

Cultural Preservation: In the context of cultural preservation, ChatGPT can assist in translating and documenting traditional texts, stories, and historical documents. This is essential for maintaining the richness of global heritage.

Research Assistant:

ChatGPT's role as a research assistant is one of its most practical and versatile applications. It serves as an accessible and knowledgeable source of information, explanations, and answers to a wide array of questions. Here's how ChatGPT excels in this capacity:

Information Retrieval: Whether you're a student, researcher, or an individual with a curious mind, ChatGPT provides a readily available information resource. By simply posing questions or prompts, you can obtain concise, reliable information on various topics. This can streamline the research process and save valuable time in information gathering.

Cross-Disciplinary Knowledge: ChatGPT's training data encompasses a wide range of subjects and domains, enabling it to answer questions related to science, history, technology, culture, and more. This cross-disciplinary knowledge makes it a valuable asset for those seeking diverse information.

Explanations and Clarifications: Beyond providing facts, ChatGPT can offer explanations and clarifications on complex topics. If you're grappling with a concept or theory, it can help break it down into more understandable terms, fostering comprehension and insight.

Problem Solving: ChatGPT is skilled at assisting with problem-solving tasks. It can provide step-by-step explanations, guidance on methodologies, and even suggest potential solutions to a wide variety of problems.

Language Assistance: If you're working on language-related projects or facing language barriers, ChatGPT can assist with grammar, vocabulary, and language translation. It aids in refining written and spoken language, making it a valuable tool for writers and language learners.

Efficiency and Accessibility: ChatGPT offers information accessibility at your fingertips. It can be used at any time and from anywhere, making it particularly helpful for quick reference or on-the-go learning.

Continuous Learning: For lifelong learners, ChatGPT is a valuable companion. Its ability to answer questions and provide explanations ensures that your quest for knowledge is continuous and convenient.

Programming Assistance:

ChatGPT's ability to assist developers in programming tasks is a valuable feature that streamlines the coding process and aids in troubleshooting. Whether you're a seasoned developer or just starting out, ChatGPT can be an invaluable resource in the following ways:

Code Generation: ChatGPT can generate code snippets in various programming languages based on your requirements and descriptions. This is particularly useful when you need to quickly implement a specific function or feature, as it can provide code templates to get you started.

Syntax Correction: For developers struggling with syntax errors or issues in their code, ChatGPT can offer suggestions and corrections. It helps identify and rectify common programming mistakes, saving time and preventing bugs.

Algorithm Assistance: If you're working on algorithm design or optimization, ChatGPT can provide insights and recommendations on the best approaches, data structures, and algorithms to use for your specific problem.

Debugging Support: Troubleshooting and debugging code can be a challenging process. ChatGPT can assist in identifying potential issues, offering tips on debugging techniques, and providing guidance on how to fix bugs in your code.

Documentation Assistance: It can help you create code comments, documentation, and explanations to make your code more readable and understandable to other developers or future versions of yourself.

Programming Language Guidance: ChatGPT is knowledgeable about various programming languages, making it versatile for developers who work in different coding environments. It can provide language-specific advice and code samples.

Conceptual Clarifications: For those learning programming concepts or dealing with complex topics, ChatGPT can break down concepts into more digestible explanations, ensuring a better understanding of the underlying principles.

Enhancing Productivity: ChatGPT's ability to quickly provide code snippets and suggestions can significantly enhance a developer's productivity, reducing the time spent on repetitive or time-consuming coding tasks.

Learning Resource: ChatGPT serves as a valuable learning resource for developers of all levels. It can answer questions, provide coding examples, and help individuals improve their programming skills over time.

ChatGPT's programming assistance goes beyond simple code generation; it serves as a dynamic programming partner capable of assisting in a wide range of software development tasks. Whether you need help with a specific coding problem or seek guidance on best practices, ChatGPT empowers developers to write cleaner, more efficient code and fosters continuous improvement in programming skills.

2.3 Limitations:

While ChatGPT is a powerful tool, it's essential to be aware of its limitations:

Lack of Understanding:

One of the most important aspects to understand about ChatGPT is that while it can produce text that often sounds plausible and coherent, it doesn't possess true understanding or context comprehension. Here's a closer look at this limitation:

Pattern-Based Responses: ChatGPT generates responses based on patterns it has learned from its vast training data. It doesn't have an inherent understanding of the information it provides. Instead, it relies on statistical associations and correlations in the data it has been exposed to.

Contextual Limitations: While ChatGPT can consider the immediate context of a conversation, it doesn't possess genuine world knowledge or the ability to retain information from one interaction to the next. Its responses are limited to the specific conversation at hand.

Inability to Reason: ChatGPT doesn't have the ability to reason, think critically, or engage in meaningful thought processes. It lacks cognitive abilities and cannot assess the accuracy or truth of the information it generates.

Plausible But Incorrect Responses: The model can sometimes generate responses that sound plausible but are factually incorrect, nonsensical, or misleading. It's important to independently verify the information it provides, especially for critical or factual matters.

Sensitivity to Input Phrasing: ChatGPT is highly sensitive to the phrasing of input. A slight change in the wording of a question or prompt can yield different results, even if the intended information is the same. This sensitivity can lead to varying or inconsistent responses.

Limited Current Knowledge: ChatGPT's knowledge is restricted to information available up to its last training data in September 2021. It may not have access to current events, developments, or information that has emerged since that date.

Absence of True Understanding: Unlike humans who can genuinely grasp concepts, build upon prior knowledge, and think critically, ChatGPT lacks the deeper comprehension and consciousness that underlie human intelligence.

Understanding this limitation is crucial when using ChatGPT. While it can be a valuable tool for generating text, answering questions, and assisting with various tasks, it should be used with care, especially when accuracy and context comprehension are essential. It's advisable to corroborate information obtained from ChatGPT through independent research and critical thinking, especially for tasks that require high levels of precision or reliability.

Bias:

A key aspect to be aware of when using ChatGPT is its potential to produce biased or inappropriate content. Understanding this limitation is essential for ensuring responsible and ethical use of the technology. Here's an in-depth exploration of this issue:

Bias in Training Data: ChatGPT is trained on a vast dataset extracted from the internet, which can contain biased or discriminatory content. The model learns from this data, and as a result, it can sometimes reflect the biases present in the training material. This can include biases related to gender, race, ethnicity, religion, and more.

Inappropriate Content: ChatGPT may occasionally generate responses that are inappropriate, offensive, or harmful. These responses can vary from mildly insensitive to deeply offensive, and they may not align with ethical or social guidelines.

Language Mimicry: ChatGPT is designed to mimic human language, and in doing so, it may sometimes replicate the bias and inappropriate language found in the training data. It's important to note that this is a reflection of the data it was trained on and not a manifestation of the model's beliefs or intentions.

The Need for Review and Moderation: To address these issues, it's crucial to review and moderate the model's output. This responsibility lies with developers, platform operators, and users who deploy ChatGPT in various applications. Reviewers and moderators play a pivotal role in flagging and addressing biased or inappropriate content.

Ethical Considerations: When using ChatGPT for applications that involve critical decision-making, such as legal or healthcare domains, it's vital to be aware of the potential bias in responses. Efforts should be made to ensure that the model's output aligns with ethical standards and does not perpetuate discrimination or harm.

Mitigation Efforts: Organizations that develop and deploy AI models like ChatGPT are continually working to reduce biases in responses. This includes refining guidelines for human reviewers during fine-tuning, improving training data curation, and employing machine learning techniques to reduce bias.

Transparency and Accountability: Promoting transparency about the capabilities and limitations of ChatGPT is essential. Users and developers should be aware of the model's potential biases and be prepared to address them proactively.

Feedback Mechanism: Platforms and users can provide feedback to organizations like OpenAI to help in the ongoing improvement of the model. This feedback loop is instrumental in identifying and rectifying issues related to bias and inappropriate content.

Recognizing and addressing bias in AI models like ChatGPT is a shared responsibility. It's incumbent upon developers, users, and organizations to actively work toward mitigating bias and ensuring that AI systems are designed and used in ways that align with ethical and social guidelines. By proactively addressing these issues, we can harness the benefits of AI while minimizing the risks associated with bias and inappropriate content.

Knowledge Cut-off:

One of the critical aspects to keep in mind when using ChatGPT is its knowledge cut-off, which is a significant limitation inherent to the model. The knowledge cut-off means that ChatGPT's understanding of the world and access to information is confined to the data it was trained on, which extends up to its last training data in September 2021. Here's a more in-depth exploration of this limitation:

Static Knowledge Base: ChatGPT's knowledge is static and does not dynamically update with real-time information or events. This means that the model is unaware of developments, news, or changes that have occurred since its last training data. Consequently, it may not provide current information on topics such as recent events, scientific discoveries, or evolving trends.

Temporal Limitation: The knowledge cut-off represents a temporal boundary, and it's crucial to be aware of this limitation when seeking information or engaging in conversations that involve recent or time-sensitive subjects. Users should exercise caution and verify information independently, especially when accuracy is paramount.

Inaccuracy of Historical Events: While ChatGPT is proficient at providing information up to its knowledge cut-off, it may not always have the most precise or up-to-date details about historical events. It's advisable to cross-reference historical facts with reliable sources, particularly when researching specific historical events.

Contextual Considerations: For discussions or tasks that rely heavily on current information, users should communicate ChatGPT's knowledge limitations to ensure that it provides contextually accurate responses. This is especially important in professional or academic contexts where accurate, up-to-date information is critical.

Ongoing Training Data Improvements: Organizations that develop AI models like ChatGPT are continually working to refine training data and models to reduce limitations related to knowledge cut-off. However, it's important for users to remain informed about the model's capabilities and limitations.

Supplementary Research: In situations where current and accurate information is required, conducting supplementary research using reliable sources remains a best practice. ChatGPT can serve as a starting point for inquiries but should not replace diligent research, especially in fields that are rapidly evolving.

By acknowledging the knowledge cut-off and understanding its implications, users can make more informed decisions about when and how to utilize ChatGPT. While the model is a valuable source of information, it's essential to use it responsibly and in conjunction with additional resources when required, to ensure the accuracy and currency of the information being sought.

Verbose Responses:

Verbose responses are one of the quirks of ChatGPT that users often encounter. This characteristic refers to the tendency of the model to provide lengthy or excessively detailed answers, sometimes including redundant information or repetitive phrases. Here's a more in-depth exploration of this aspect:

Pattern-Based Generation: ChatGPT generates responses based on patterns it has learned from its training data. In some cases, it may overemphasize specific patterns or phrases, leading to verbose responses that contain more information than necessary.

Lack of Conciseness: Unlike human communication, ChatGPT doesn't possess the natural ability to provide concise and focused answers. It may, at times, over-explain concepts or issues, leading to responses that are longer than what's needed to address the query effectively.

User-Friendly Language: The model is trained to be user-friendly and provide informative responses, which can occasionally result in explanations that border on verbosity. While this can be helpful in certain contexts, it may not always align with a user's preference for brevity.

Sensitivity to Input: ChatGPT's responses are highly sensitive to the phrasing of the input. Slight variations in how a question is posed can lead to varying levels of verbosity in the responses.

Balancing Act: For developers and users, striking a balance between comprehensive responses and concise ones is essential. This may involve reformulating queries or explicitly requesting shorter answers when desired.

Review and Editing: In professional or communication-sensitive contexts, reviewing and editing ChatGPT's responses for conciseness can be a prudent practice. This helps ensure that the information presented is clear and to the point.

User Feedback: Providing feedback to organizations like OpenAI can help improve the model's ability to generate more concise responses. User input assists in fine-tuning and enhancing the model's communication style.

Understanding ChatGPT's tendency for verbose responses allows users to adapt their interactions with the model to their specific needs. While the model aims to be informative, it's advisable to review and refine responses when clarity, brevity, or a specific style of communication is required, ensuring that the output aligns with the user's communication goals.

Sensitivity to Input:

ChatGPT's sensitivity to input phrasing is a notable characteristic of the model that users should be aware of. This sensitivity means that small changes in the way a question or prompt is formulated can lead to varying or even contrasting responses. Here's a closer look at this aspect:

Language Patterns: ChatGPT's responses are generated based on patterns and associations it has learned from its training data. It doesn't possess true understanding but instead relies on recognizing patterns and language structures. As a result, slight differences in input phrasing can lead to different responses.

Synonyms and Word Choices: Variations in synonyms, word choices, or the order of words can all influence the way ChatGPT interprets a question. For example, asking "What's the weather like today?" and "Tell me about today's weather" might yield similar but not identical responses.

Context Shift: A change in phrasing can also affect the context of the conversation. Even a subtle shift in how a question is posed may lead to the model interpreting the context differently, which in turn influences its response.

Conciseness vs. Verbosity: Adjusting the level of detail or verbosity in a question can prompt ChatGPT to provide more or less detailed responses. Users can use this sensitivity to their advantage by requesting responses of varying depth or complexity.

Consistency Challenges: This sensitivity can be challenging for users who expect consistent responses from the model. It's important to be mindful of the potential for variability in responses due to minor changes in input.

Adapting to Specific Needs: Users who are aware of this sensitivity can adapt their interactions with the model to better suit their specific needs. By experimenting with different phrasings, they can elicit the kind of responses they are looking for.

Clarifying Ambiguity: When faced with ambiguous queries, ChatGPT may generate multiple possible interpretations. Users can then clarify their intent to get the most accurate response.

Inappropriate Content:

The potential for ChatGPT to generate inappropriate or offensive content, despite mitigation efforts, is an important consideration when using the model. This limitation stems from the model's ability to mimic human language, which can occasionally lead to responses that include inappropriate language or offensive material. Let's delve deeper into this aspect:

Training Data Challenges: ChatGPT is trained on a vast dataset that includes content from the internet. This dataset, while diverse and comprehensive, also contains instances of inappropriate, harmful, or offensive content. The model, in turn, may occasionally reflect this content in its responses.

Mimicry of Human Speech: The model's design emphasizes the mimicry of human language, and this includes replicating the patterns and phrasing it encounters in its training data. Consequently, ChatGPT may generate responses that sound inappropriate or offensive, even though it lacks the intent to offend.

Content Moderation: Organizations like OpenAI put significant effort into content moderation to minimize the generation of harmful or inappropriate content. However, due to the volume of interactions and the evolving nature of language, some instances may still bypass automated moderation.

User Responsibility: Users and platform operators have a role to play in addressing this limitation. It's important to review and moderate the model's responses, ensuring that the output aligns with ethical and social guidelines. This can involve setting up content filters, guidelines, or manual review processes.

Continual Improvement: Organizations continue to work on improving models like ChatGPT to reduce instances of inappropriate content. Feedback from users plays a vital role in refining the model and enhancing its content moderation capabilities.

Ethical Usage: Responsible use of ChatGPT is essential. Users should refrain from attempting to provoke the model into generating offensive content and should apply ethical guidelines when deploying the technology in applications that interact with a broad audience.

Recognizing the potential for inappropriate content is crucial in ensuring that ChatGPT is used responsibly and safely. By understanding this limitation and actively addressing it through moderation and guidelines, users can harness the benefits of AI while minimizing the risk of generating harmful or offensive material.

GPT-3 Architecture:

ChatGPT is built upon the foundation of the GPT-3.5 architecture, an evolution of the renowned GPT-3 model. To better understand ChatGPT, it's essential to explore the architecture that powers it. Here's a comprehensive look at the GPT-3.5 architecture:

Generative Pre-trained Transformer (GPT): The acronym 'GPT' stands for 'Generative Pre-trained Transformer.' This name encapsulates the essence of the model. Let's break down these components:

Generative: The term 'generative' signifies the model's ability to generate text. It can create human-like text, making it suitable for tasks such as text completion, text generation, and natural language understanding.

Pre-trained: 'Pre-trained' implies that the model is initially trained on a vast dataset before being fine-tuned for specific tasks. During pre-training, the model learns the statistical patterns and associations in the data, enabling it to understand and generate text effectively.

Transformer: The 'Transformer' architecture is a critical component of GPT. Transformers are deep learning models designed to handle sequences of data, such as sentences or paragraphs. This architecture, with its self-attention mechanisms, is highly effective in capturing contextual relationships within text.

Massive Neural Network: GPT-3.5 is characterized by its vast neural network, which consists of a staggering 175 billion parameters. Parameters are the learnable components of the model that store information and govern its behaviour. The sheer scale of GPT-3.5's neural network contributes to its ability to understand and generate text at an advanced level.

Language Modelling: The core function of the GPT-3.5 architecture is language modelling. It excels at understanding and generating human-like text by modelling the statistical patterns and relationships within the text data it has been exposed to during training.

Evolution from GPT-3: GPT-3.5 represents an advancement from the earlier GPT-3 model. It builds upon the capabilities of GPT-3, which itself had 175 billion parameters. The evolution involves fine-tuning and adjustments to enhance the model's performance, accuracy, and safety.

State-of-the-Art Language Model: GPT-3.5 is recognized as one of the most advanced language models in existence. Its vast parameter count, coupled with the transformer architecture, enables it to perform exceptionally well in a variety of natural language processing tasks, ranging from text generation to text understanding.

Fine-Tuning: After the initial pre-training on a diverse dataset, GPT-3.5 undergoes fine-tuning to tailor its behaviour for specific use cases and safety standards. Fine-tuning is a crucial phase in the development of the model, enabling customization for various applications.

GPT-3.5's architecture underpins its impressive text generation and understanding capabilities. It serves as the foundation for ChatGPT, allowing ChatGPT to engage in dynamic conversations, answer questions, generate content, and assist users across a wide range of applications. Understanding the architecture is essential for users and developers to leverage the model effectively and appreciate its advanced language processing capabilities.

Knowledge Cut-off (September 2021):

The knowledge cut-off is a fundamental limitation that applies to GPT-3.5, including ChatGPT. Understanding this limitation is crucial for users who rely on the model for accurate and current information. Here's a comprehensive explanation of the knowledge cut-off and its implications:

Temporal Boundary: The knowledge cut-off establishes a temporal boundary beyond which ChatGPT does not possess information. This boundary is defined by the date of the last training data, which, in the case of GPT-3.5, is September 2021. In practical terms, this means that the model's knowledge is limited to information that was available and accessible up to that date.

Static Knowledge Base: ChatGPT's knowledge base remains static and does not dynamically update with real-time data or events. As a result, the model is not aware of developments, news, discoveries, or trends that have occurred since its knowledge cut-off date.

Accuracy and Relevance: When using ChatGPT for information retrieval or discussions, it's important to bear in mind that the model's responses may not be entirely accurate or relevant to recent events. If you inquire about current news, for instance, the model's responses may be outdated or incorrect.

Historical Context: For historical facts and events that predate the knowledge cut-off, ChatGPT can be a valuable resource. It can provide detailed information on historical topics, making it a useful tool for historical research or inquiries.

Cross-Verification: In situations where up-to-date and accurate information is vital, it's advisable to cross-verify information obtained from ChatGPT with reliable, current sources. This is particularly important for news, current events, scientific discoveries, and rapidly evolving fields.

Ongoing Learning: Users should approach ChatGPT with the awareness that its responses are based on information up to September 2021. This understanding allows for more precise interactions with the model, helping users seek information and engage in discussions within the context of its knowledge boundary.

Model Advancements: It's worth noting that developers and organizations continuously work to improve models like ChatGPT. Future iterations of the model may have updated knowledge, but it's essential to be mindful of the current knowledge cut-off when using the model.

Chapter 3: Basic Usage

Section 3.1: Starting a Conversation with ChatGPT

Starting a conversation with ChatGPT is a straightforward process, whether you're using a web interface, an API, or a dedicated application. Here's a step-by-step guide on how to initiate a conversation and best practices for effective communication:

Step 1: Access ChatGPT

- Open the platform or application through which you access ChatGPT. This could be a website, a mobile app, or a software integrated with the API.

Step 2: Begin a Conversation

- Click on the "Start Chat" or "New Conversation" button to initiate a chat session with ChatGPT.

Step 3: Greet and Introduce Your Query

- Start your conversation by greeting ChatGPT. For instance, "Hello, ChatGPT!" or "Hi there!"

- Introduce your query or topic clearly and concisely. For example, "Can you help me with a recipe for lasagne?" or "I need assistance with a coding problem."

Step 4: Pose Questions and Provide Context

- Ask questions one at a time, providing context if necessary. This helps ChatGPT understand your request. For instance, "What are the key ingredients for lasagne?" or "I'm getting an error message in my code, can you assist with debugging?"

Step 5: Interact and Follow Up

- Engage in a dynamic conversation by responding to ChatGPT's answers and asking follow-up questions. Maintain a conversational flow to gather the information you need.

Section 3.2: Tips for Effective Communication

Effective communication with ChatGPT can enhance the quality of responses and your overall experience. Here are some tips:

Be clear and specific: Provide clear and specific details in your questions or requests to help ChatGPT understand your intent.

Use Concise Language: While ChatGPT can handle verbosity, being concise in your queries can lead to more focused responses.

Ask One Question at a Time: To avoid confusion and ensure accurate responses, ask one question or make one request in each message.

Clarify Ambiguity: If ChatGPT's response is unclear or you encounter ambiguity, don't hesitate to ask for clarification.

Set Expectations: Clearly communicate your expectations. For instance, if you want a brief answer or a detailed explanation, mention it in your request.

Engage Actively: Maintain an interactive conversation by responding to ChatGPT's answers and asking follow-up questions for more context.

Section 3.3: Common Use Cases

ChatGPT is a versatile tool with various use cases. Here are some common scenarios where ChatGPT can be of help:

Generating Content: Use ChatGPT to generate text for articles, reports, marketing materials, or any written content. Share the topic and any specific requirements to get started.

Brainstorming Ideas: Seek creative inspiration by discussing your project or problem with ChatGPT. It can offer suggestions, ideas, or alternative approaches.

Answering Questions: Use ChatGPT as a knowledge resource for answering questions related to history, science, technology, or general knowledge.

Programming Assistance: Get code snippets, debugging help, or explanations for programming-related issues.

Learning and Education: Use ChatGPT to assist with explanations, provide language translations, or answer questions for educational purposes.

Language Translation: Utilize ChatGPT for translating text between languages, breaking down language barriers, and facilitating communication.

Research Assistance: Seek information, explanations, or references on a wide range of topics, making ChatGPT your virtual research assistant.

By following these steps and tips, you can start productive conversations with ChatGPT and leverage it for various tasks, making the most of its capabilities in content generation, brainstorming, answering questions, and much more.

Chapter 4: Advanced Features

Section 4.1: Customizing Responses

Customizing responses in ChatGPT can add a layer of personalization to your interactions. Here's how to use this advanced feature effectively:

Custom Prompts: Instead of using generic prompts like "Translate the following text to French," you can customize your prompts with a personal touch. For example, "I need a French translation for this text: 'Hello, world!'" Adding context and a personal touch to your prompts can yield more relevant responses.

Controlling Output Length: You can specify the length of the response you want. For instance, if you're generating text for a Twitter post, you might want it to be concise. On the other hand, if you're writing an essay, you can request longer responses.

Tone and Style Customization: ChatGPT can generate responses in different tones, such as formal, casual, or informative. You can specify the tone you prefer to ensure the response aligns with your communication style or the requirements of your project.

Section 4.2: Setting the Tone or Style of Responses

ChatGPT is capable of adjusting the tone and style of its responses to match your preferences or the context of the conversation:

Formal Language: If you're working on a professional document or correspondence, you can instruct ChatGPT to use formal language and tone to maintain a business-appropriate style.

Casual Language: For more relaxed and informal interactions, ChatGPT can be directed to use a casual style, making the conversation feel friendly and approachable.

Informative Style: In scenarios where you require detailed explanations, you can specify that you want responses in an informative or educational style, ensuring a deep and comprehensive answer.

Section 4.3: Using System Messages

System messages are a powerful tool to guide the conversation and set expectations. Here's how to make the most of this feature:

Introduction and Context: Start your conversation with a system message to introduce the context or guidelines for the conversation. For instance, you can use a system message to set the stage for a coding assistance session by stating, "Let's work on debugging the code."

Role Play: In role-playing scenarios, you can use system messages to establish the characters and roles within the conversation. For example, in a customer support simulation, you can set the system message to "You are the customer, and I am the support agent."

Scenario Definitions: Define the scenario or context explicitly. If you're brainstorming ideas for a marketing campaign, you can use a system message like "Let's brainstorm creative concepts for our upcoming marketing campaign."

Redirect or Clarify: If the conversation veers off track or if ChatGPT provides an unclear response, a system message can be used to redirect the conversation or request clarification, ensuring that the dialogue remains on point.

By leveraging these advanced features, you can fine-tune your interactions with ChatGPT, ensuring that the responses align with your style, context, and requirements. Customizing responses, setting the tone, and using system messages empower you to have more meaningful and tailored conversations with the model, whether it's for professional documents, creative writing, educational content, or any other use case.

Chapter 5: Best Practices

Section 5.1: Obtaining Accurate and Relevant Information

Obtaining accurate and relevant information from ChatGPT is essential for making the most of the tool. Here are some tips for achieving this:

Be Specific: When asking questions or making requests, be as specific as possible. Clear and precise inquiries help ChatGPT provide more accurate responses.

Cross-Verification: Always cross-verify information obtained from ChatGPT with reliable sources, especially for critical or factual matters. This is particularly important in academic, professional, and research contexts.

Check Dates: If you're seeking time-sensitive information, be aware of ChatGPT's knowledge cut-off (September 2021) and clarify if you need recent data.

Request References: When ChatGPT provides factual information, ask for references or sources to support its claims. This can help ensure the credibility of the information.

Use Descriptive Prompts: Customize your prompts to include context and details, which can lead to more targeted responses. For instance, instead of "Tell me about World War II," try "Provide a concise overview of the key events of World War II."

Section 5.2: Ethical Considerations and Responsible Use

Responsible and ethical use of ChatGPT is of utmost importance. Here are ethical considerations and tips for responsible use:

Avoid Harm: Do not use ChatGPT to generate or spread harmful, inappropriate, or offensive content. Always review and moderate the model's responses in applications with broader audiences.

Respect Privacy: Do not share sensitive or private information with ChatGPT. It's important to remember that the model is a tool and not a trustworthy entity.

Be Transparent: If you're using ChatGPT in a professional or customer service capacity, clearly communicate that you're interacting with an AI and not a human agent. Transparency builds trust and sets appropriate expectations.

Educational Use: In educational settings, encourage students to use ChatGPT as a supplementary resource and emphasize the importance of independent research and critical thinking.

Compliance with Guidelines: If you're using ChatGPT in a regulated industry or organization, ensure that your interactions align with industry guidelines, compliance standards, and ethical codes.

Section 5.3: Addressing Potential Biases

Addressing potential biases in ChatGPT is a critical aspect of responsible use. Here are ways to mitigate biases:

Content Moderation: Implement content moderation processes to filter out inappropriate, biased, or offensive responses. This helps ensure that the output aligns with ethical and social guidelines.

Review and Edit: In professional or communication-sensitive contexts, review and edit the model's responses for bias, clarity, and appropriateness.

Bias Detection Tools: Explore the use of bias detection tools and libraries to identify and rectify biased language or responses.

Feedback Loop: Provide feedback to the organization or platform operating ChatGPT to help improve the model's ability to reduce bias and generate more balanced content.

Guidelines for Reviewers: Organizations fine-tuning the model should establish clear guidelines for human reviewers, emphasizing the importance of addressing and avoiding biases in responses.

By adhering to these best practices, users can obtain accurate and reliable information from ChatGPT, use the tool responsibly in various contexts, and actively contribute to the mitigation of biases. Responsible use and ethical considerations are integral to harnessing the benefits of AI models while minimizing potential risks.

Chapter 6: Real-World Applications

ChatGPT, powered by the GPT-3.5 architecture, offers versatile capabilities that find applications across numerous industries and fields. Here, we showcase real-world examples of how ChatGPT can be applied to solve challenges, improve efficiency, and provide innovative solutions:

Section 6.1: Healthcare

1. Medical Assistance: ChatGPT can assist medical professionals by providing explanations of medical terms, helping with diagnosis research, and offering insights into the latest medical research and treatments.

2. Telemedicine: In telemedicine platforms, ChatGPT can serve as a virtual assistant for patients, answering health-related questions, scheduling appointments, and providing medication reminders.

3. Healthcare Chatbots: Healthcare organizations can use ChatGPT to power chatbots that guide patients through symptom assessments, direct them to the right services, and offer preliminary medical advice.

Section 6.2: Education

1. Virtual Tutors: ChatGPT can act as a virtual tutor, offering explanations and clarifications to students on various subjects, helping with homework, and encouraging engagement in learning.

2. Automated Essay Scoring: Educational institutions can use ChatGPT to automate essay scoring, providing instant feedback on students' writing assignments.

3. Language Learning: ChatGPT can assist language learners by providing translations, explanations of grammar rules, and conversation practice.

Section 6.3: Content Creation and Marketing

1. Content Generation: Content creators can utilize ChatGPT to generate articles, blog posts, and marketing materials, helping to streamline content production.

2. Social Media Posts: Marketers can use ChatGPT to draft engaging and creative social media posts, saving time and enhancing their online presence.

3. Email Marketing: Automated email marketing campaigns can benefit from ChatGPT's ability to craft personalized and compelling email content.

Section 6.4: Customer Support and Service

1. AI Chatbots: ChatGPT can power AI chatbots in customer support, offering round-the-clock assistance, addressing common queries, and escalating complex issues to human agents.

2. Interactive FAQs: Websites and applications can implement interactive FAQs powered by ChatGPT, enhancing user experiences and helping users find answers efficiently.

3. Automated Ticketing: ChatGPT can automate ticket creation and routing in customer service systems, improving the efficiency of issue resolution.

Section 6.5: Research and Data Analysis

1. Data Extraction: Researchers and analysts can use ChatGPT to extract insights from large datasets, helping identify trends, correlations, and patterns.

2. Literature Review: ChatGPT can assist in conducting literature reviews, summarizing research papers, and generating annotated bibliographies.

3. Market Research: In market research, ChatGPT can help generate surveys, analyse results, and provide insights into consumer behaviour and preferences.

Section 6.6: Software Development

1. Code Generation: Developers can leverage ChatGPT to generate code snippets, offer debugging suggestions, and assist in solving programming challenges.

2. Documentation: ChatGPT can help create software documentation, offering clear explanations of APIs, functions, and processes.

3. Stack Overflow Support: ChatGPT can provide answers to developers' queries on platforms like Stack Overflow, increasing the accessibility of information.

Section 6.7: Translation and Multilingual Communication

1. Translation Services: ChatGPT's language translation capabilities can be used in e-commerce, tourism, and international business to facilitate communication between speakers of different languages.

2. Multilingual Customer Support: Organizations with a global presence can use ChatGPT for multilingual customer support, ensuring that queries in various languages are addressed effectively.

3. Cultural Understanding: ChatGPT can assist in cross-cultural communication by providing insights into cultural norms, etiquette, and best practices when interacting with individuals from different backgrounds.

These real-world examples illustrate the adaptability of ChatGPT across diverse domains. Its ability to generate content, provide assistance, and engage in conversations makes it a valuable tool for enhancing productivity, streamlining processes, and improving user experiences in numerous industries and fields.

Chapter 7: Troubleshooting and FAQs

In this chapter, we address common issues that users might encounter when interacting with ChatGPT and provide answers to frequently asked questions to help you make the most of your experience:

Section 7.1: Common Issues and Solutions

1. Verbose Responses: If you receive overly verbose responses, try rephrasing your questions to request more concise answers. Alternatively, you can specify that you want shorter, to-the-point responses.

2. Lack of Clarity: If a response is unclear, consider asking ChatGPT for clarification by providing more context or rephrasing your query.

3. Bias in Responses: If you encounter biased or inappropriate content, remember to review and moderate the model's responses. Implement content filters and guidelines to reduce the likelihood of biased responses.

4. Sensitivity to Input: To obtain consistent responses, ensure that your queries are clear and specific. Slight variations in phrasing can yield different results, so be precise in your questions.

5. Knowledge Cut-off: When inquiring about recent information or events, acknowledge ChatGPT's knowledge cut-off (September 2021) and cross-verify data with up-to-date sources when needed.

Section 7.2: Frequently Asked Questions

1. Is ChatGPT the same as human intelligence?

- No, ChatGPT is an AI language model that doesn't possess human-like intelligence. It generates responses based on patterns in its training data but lacks genuine understanding.

2. Can ChatGPT provide real-time or updated information?

- No, ChatGPT's knowledge is static, limited to information available up to its last training data in September 2021. It cannot provide real-time or updated information.

3. How can I reduce biased or inappropriate responses from ChatGPT?

- Implement content moderation, review and edit responses, provide feedback to improve the model's behaviour, and set clear guidelines for using ChatGPT in your applications.

4. Can I use ChatGPT for academic or professional research?

- Yes, ChatGPT can be a valuable resource for research, offering explanations, references, and insights. However, it's essential to cross-verify information with credible sources for accuracy.

5. What are some best practices for more effective interactions with ChatGPT?

- Be specific in your queries, use concise language, and ask one question at a time. Set expectations for response length, tone, and style. Review and moderate responses for accuracy and appropriateness.

6. Is ChatGPT a secure platform for sensitive or private information?

- No, it's not advisable to share sensitive or private information with ChatGPT. Always exercise caution and refrain from sharing confidential data.

7. Can I use ChatGPT in my business or organization?

- Yes, ChatGPT can be integrated into various business applications for customer support, content generation, and more. Ensure that usage aligns with your organization's ethical guidelines.

8. How can I customize ChatGPT's responses to my needs?

- You can customize prompts, control response length, and specify the tone and style you desire. Use system messages to set the context and role for the conversation.

By addressing common issues and answering frequently asked questions, this chapter equips users with practical solutions and insights for a more effective and informed experience when using ChatGPT.

Chapter 8: Future Developments

The field of AI and ChatGPT technology is continually evolving, driven by ongoing research and advancements. Here, we explore future developments and updates in AI and ChatGPT, along with how users can stay informed about these changes:

Section 8.1: Upcoming AI Developments

1. Improved Accuracy: Future iterations of AI models like ChatGPT are likely to focus on improving accuracy, reducing biases, and enhancing language understanding. This means more precise and context-aware responses.

2. Dynamic Learning: AI models may incorporate dynamic learning mechanisms, allowing them to adapt to emerging trends and updates. This could enable the model to provide more up-to-date information beyond its knowledge cut-off date.

3. Specialized Models: AI models tailored for specific industries or applications may become more prevalent, offering optimized performance and relevance for users in those domains.

4. Expanded Multimodal Capabilities: Future AI models may combine text with other modes of data, such as images and audio, for more comprehensive and interactive responses.

Section 8.2: Updates to ChatGPT

1. Knowledge Updates: Future updates to ChatGPT could include ways to access and integrate more recent knowledge, enabling it to provide information on events and developments occurring after its last training data.

2. Advanced Customization: Users may gain more control over the customization of responses, including specifying complex styles and tones tailored to their specific needs.

3. Enhanced Content Moderation: Updates may refine the content moderation system to minimize biased, inappropriate, or unsafe responses.

4. Wider Integration: ChatGPT could become more integrated into various applications and platforms, expanding its reach across industries.

Section 8.3: How Users Can Stay Informed

To stay informed about developments in AI and ChatGPT technology, users can take the following steps:

1. Follow AI Research Organizations: Keep an eye on the latest research publications and announcements from organizations like OpenAI, which regularly provide insights into AI advancements.

2. Join AI Communities: Participate in AI and ChatGPT communities, forums, and social media groups where researchers and enthusiasts discuss the latest developments.

3. Regularly Check Updates: Visit the official websites of AI service providers and platforms to check for updates, release notes, and news related to AI models like ChatGPT.

4. Read Tech News: Tech news outlets and publications often cover AI advancements and their real-world applications, offering a broad view of industry developments.

5. Participate in Beta Testing: If available, consider participating in beta testing programs for new AI technologies to gain early access and first-hand experience with upcoming features.

6. Follow AI Experts: Follow AI researchers, experts, and practitioners on social media platforms, where they often share insights and updates on AI technology.

7. Subscribe to Newsletters: Subscribe to newsletters and mailing lists from AI organizations and research institutions to receive regular updates and news.

8. Engage in Webinars and Conferences: Attend webinars, conferences, and seminars dedicated to AI and natural language processing to hear from experts and researchers.

Chapter 9: References and Resources

For users interested in delving deeper into the world of AI and ChatGPT, there is a wealth of recommended reading, articles, and resources available to help you expand your knowledge and expertise. Here is a list of valuable references and resources to explore:

Section 9.1: Recommended Reading

1. "Artificial Intelligence: A Guide to Intelligent Systems" by Michael Negnevitsky: This book provides a comprehensive introduction to AI concepts, including natural language processing, and is suitable for beginners.

2. "Deep Learning" by Ian Goodfellow and Yoshua Bengio: A comprehensive resource for understanding the deep learning techniques that underpin models like GPT-3.5.

3. "Language Models are Few-Shot Learners" by Tom B. Brown et al. (OpenAI): The original paper on GPT-3 that introduced the concept of few-shot learning, offering insight into the model's capabilities.

4. "The Next Decade in AI: Four Steps Towards Robust Artificial Intelligence" by Gary Marcus and Ernest Davis: A thought-provoking article that discusses the future of AI development and its challenges.

Section 9.2: Articles and Blogs

1. OpenAI Blog: OpenAI's official blog is a valuable source for updates, research papers, and insights into AI models, including ChatGPT.

2. Towards Data Science: A Medium publication with a wide range of articles on AI, machine learning, and natural language processing.

3. MIT Technology Review: A reputable source for news and analysis on AI trends and developments.

4. Synced Review: A hub for AI and machine learning news, offering articles, research summaries, and expert insights.

Section 9.3: Online Courses and Tutorials

1. Coursera's "Deep Learning Specialization" by Andrew Ng: This course series offers a comprehensive introduction to deep learning, which is essential for understanding AI models like ChatGPT.

2. Fast.ai's "Practical Deep Learning for Coders": A practical, hands-on approach to deep learning and natural language processing, with a focus on code implementation.

3. Stanford's "Natural Language Processing with Deep Learning" course: A deep dive into NLP concepts and technologies.

Section 9.4: AI Communities and Forums

1. Reddit's r/MachineLearning: A vibrant community where AI enthusiasts, researchers, and professionals discuss AI topics and share valuable resources.

2. Stack Exchange's AI Stack Exchange: A Q&A platform for AI and machine learning where you can ask and answer questions.

Section 9.5: Research Journals

1. Journal of Artificial Intelligence Research (JAIR): An open-access journal publishing high-quality AI research articles.

2. Journal of Machine Learning Research (JMLR): A peer-reviewed journal that covers research in machine learning and related fields.

Section 9.6: AI Research Organizations

1. OpenAI: The organization behind GPT models, offering research papers, blog posts, and documentation on their models and technologies.

2. Google AI: Google's AI research division, which publishes research papers and offers resources on various AI topics.

3. Microsoft Research AI: Microsoft's research division focused on AI, with valuable resources and publications.

Chapter 10: Glossary

Understanding AI-related terminology is crucial for effectively engaging with AI systems and staying informed about the field. Here is a glossary of key AI-related terms and concepts to assist users in comprehending the terminology:

1. Artificial Intelligence (AI): The development of computer systems that can perform tasks that typically require human intelligence, such as visual perception, speech recognition, decision-making, and problem-solving.

2. Machine Learning (ML): A subset of AI that focuses on the development of algorithms and models that enable computers to learn from and make predictions or decisions based on data.

3. Deep Learning: A subfield of machine learning that uses artificial neural networks with many layers (deep neural networks) to process and understand data.

4. Neural Network: A computational model inspired by the structure and function of the human brain, used in deep learning for tasks such as image and speech recognition.

5. Natural Language Processing (NLP): The AI field focused on the interaction between computers and human language, including tasks like language generation, translation, and sentiment analysis.

6. Supervised Learning: A machine learning paradigm where models are trained on labelled data, learning to make predictions or classifications based on input-output pairs.

7. Unsupervised Learning: Machine learning that deals with unlabelled data, where algorithms discover patterns or structure in the data without predefined labels.

8. Reinforcement Learning: A type of machine learning where agents learn to make decisions by taking actions in an environment, receiving rewards or punishments in response.

9. Generative Model: A type of AI model that can generate new data, such as text, images, or music, often used in creative tasks.

10. Transformer: A neural network architecture used in many modern NLP models, including GPT (Generative Pre-trained Transformer), known for its ability to understand and generate human-like text.

11. Fine-Tuning: The process of adapting a pre-trained model to specific tasks or domains by training it further on task-specific data.

12. Bias: In AI, bias refers to the presence of unfair or discriminatory outcomes in algorithms or models, often due to biased training data.

13. Knowledge Cut-off: The date at which an AI model's training data ends, beyond which it does not have access to information, resulting in a static knowledge base.

14. Few-Shot Learning: A machine learning approach that allows models to make accurate predictions or generate content with minimal examples or input.

15. GPT-3.5: A model based on the GPT (Generative Pre-trained Transformer) architecture with 175 billion parameters, known for its conversational and text generation abilities.

16. Bias Mitigation: Techniques and strategies used to reduce or eliminate biases in AI models, ensuring fairness and ethical behaviour.

17. Content Moderation: The process of reviewing and filtering user-generated content, such as text, images, or videos, to remove inappropriate or harmful material.

18. API (Application Programming Interface): A set of rules and protocols that allows different software applications to communicate with each other.

19. NLP Application: Any software or system that utilizes natural language processing for tasks like chatbots, language translation, sentiment analysis, and text generation.

20. Knowledge Transfer: The process of transferring knowledge from one AI model to another, often to improve the performance of the latter.

Understanding these AI-related terms and concepts will help users engage with AI systems more effectively and navigate the ever-evolving landscape of artificial intelligence and machine learning.

Conclusion

In this comprehensive guidebook, we've explored the fascinating world of AI, with a particular focus on ChatGPT, a powerful language model based on the GPT-3.5 architecture. We've covered a wide array of topics, from understanding the technology behind ChatGPT to its practical applications, ethical considerations, and future developments in the field of AI.

Throughout the chapters, you've gained insights into the capabilities and limitations of ChatGPT, learned best practices for using it effectively, and discovered real-world applications across various industries. We've equipped you with a glossary of essential AI-related terms and resources to further your knowledge.

As AI continues to shape the world we live in, the role of ChatGPT and similar models is becoming increasingly significant, making it essential to stay informed and make the most of these powerful tools. However, it's equally important to approach them responsibly, considering ethical considerations and potential biases.

We encourage you to provide feedback, suggestions, or any questions you might have. Your input is invaluable in improving this guidebook and ensuring that it remains a relevant and valuable resource for users like you. AI technology is evolving rapidly, and your feedback helps us keep pace with the latest developments and trends.

Thank you for choosing this guidebook as your companion in the world of AI and ChatGPT. We look forward to your insights and hope this resource serves you well in your AI journey. Stay curious, stay engaged, and keep exploring the exciting frontiers of artificial intelligence!

Don't miss out!

Visit the website below and you can sign up to receive emails whenever PA BOOKS publishes a new book. There's no charge and no obligation.

https://books2read.com/r/B-A-STTAB-SURPC

BOOKS 2 READ

Connecting independent readers to independent writers.

Also by PA BOOKS

Hogan's Key
Kimberly & the Five Strange Goldfishes
The Enchanted Library
The Misadventures of Pirate Pete
From Wheel To Web: 40 Remarkable Inventions
Once Upon A Sleepy Time
The Global Game - The Evolution Of Football
Strides To Success: A Beginner's Guide to Running
The ChatGPT Handbook

www.ingramcontent.com/pod-product-compliance
Lightning Source LLC
Chambersburg PA
CBHW021324160726
47994CB00004B/1600